THE REAL
MOTHER GOOSE BOOK OF
CHRISTMAS CAROLS

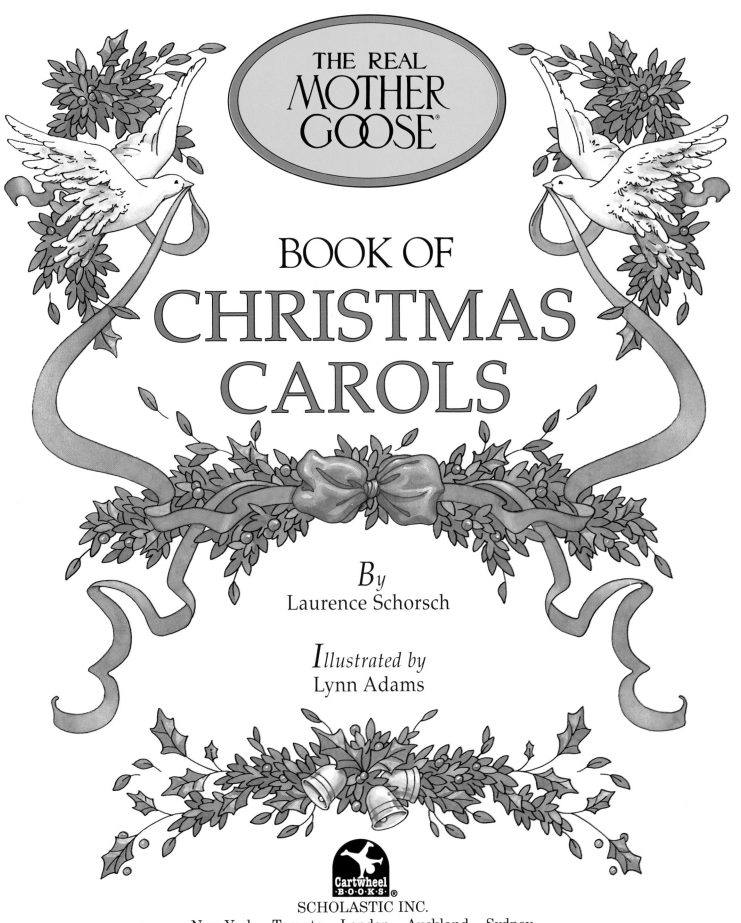

THE REAL MOTHER GOOSE®

BOOK OF

CHRISTMAS CAROLS

By
Laurence Schorsch

Illustrated by
Lynn Adams

Cartwheel
B·O·O·K·S®
SCHOLASTIC INC.
New York   Toronto   London   Auckland   Sydney
Mexico City   New Delhi   Hong Kong   Buenos Aires

Designed by Tom Koken
Music arranged by Robert FitzSimons

12 11 10 9 8 7 6 5 4 3 2 1   4 5 6 7 8 9/0
                    Printed in Singapore   46

First compilation printing, September 2004

ISBN 0-7607-5883-2

This edition created exclusively for Barnes & Noble, Inc.
2004 Barnes & Noble Books

CONTENTS

INTRODUCTION

A carol was originally a circular dance, and many of the older carols are lively dance tunes. Words were later added to the music to go along with the dancing. When the church banned dancing, people continued to sing the songs, even though they were not allowed to dance to them. The words were not always about Christian subjects, and many of them were related to old pagan customs. This soon caused the church to ban carols altogether. But carols survived outside the church, and became a kind of religious folk music.

St. Francis of Assisi is credited with helping to bring carols back into the church. In 1223 he got permission from the Pope to hold a midnight mass in a nativity stable with live animals in the town of Grecchio, Italy. Some of his friars wrote carol-like songs which the church approved of.

Another thing that helped to make carols acceptable to the church was their use in miracle plays. These plays were based on stories from the Bible that told about the life, death, and resurrection of Christ. They were performed during major religious festivals. And so, carols were once again allowed in the church.

Later, during the Reformation, carols were banned by some Protestants. Those that did allow singing decided that the words had to be about religious subjects. In England, the Puritans banned all carols, and in 1647 even the celebration of Christmas was banned! Since many parts of America were settled by Puritans, it took a long time for carols to become acceptable here. In the nineteenth century, people became interested in singing carols again. Many old carols were rediscovered and many new ones were written. A lot of these have remained popular ever since.

HARK! THE HERALD ANGELS SING

The words to this carol were written by Charles Wesley who, with his brother, John, started the Methodist church in 1729. More than a hundred years after the hymn was first published, the words were set to music that the great composer Felix Mendelssohn wrote to commemorate the 400th anniversary of the invention of printing. The carol joyfully celebrates the birth of Christ, "born that man no more may die."

Charles Wesley

Felix Mendelssohn

Merrily

Hark! the he-rald an-gels sing,_ Glo-ry to the new-born King; Peace on

earth and mer-cy mild, - God and sin-ners re-con-ciled: Joy-ful, all ye na-tions,

rise,_ Join the tri-umph of the skies,_ With the~an-ge-lic host pro-claim Christ is_

born in Beth-le-hem: Hark! the he-rald an-gels sing, Glo-ry_ to the new-born King.

1. Hark! the herald angels sing,
Glory to the new-born King;
Peace on earth and mercy mild,
God and sinners reconciled:
Joyful, all ye nations, rise,
Join the triumph of the skies,
With the angelic host proclaim
Christ is born in Bethlehem:
Hark! the herald angels sing,
Glory to the new-born King.

2. Christ, by highest heaven adored;
Christ, the everlasting Lord;
Late in time behold him come,
Offspring of a Virgin's womb;
Veiled in flesh the Godhead see,
Hail the incarnate Deity!
Pleased as man with man to dwell,
Jesus, our Emmanuel:
Hark! the herald angels sing,
Glory to the new-born King.

3. Hail the heaven-born Prince of Peace!
Hail the Sun of Righteousness!
Light and life to all he brings,
Risen with healing in his wings;
Mild he lays his glory by,
Born that man no more may die,
Born to raise the sons of earth,
Born to give them second birth:
Hark! the herald angels sing,
Glory to the new-born King.

4. Come, desire of nations, come!
Fix us in thy humble home;
Rise, the woman's conquering seed,
Bruise in us the serpent's head.
Adam's likeness now efface,
Stamp thy image in its place;
Second Adam from above,
Reinstate us in thy love:
Hark! the herald angels sing,
Glory to the new-born King.

13

IT CAME UPON A MIDNIGHT CLEAR

The words to this carol were written in 1849 by Edmund Hamilton Sears, a Unitarian minister from Massachusetts. The music is by the composer Richard S. Willis and was originally written for another carol. In the early verses, Sears describes a world full of suffering where men do not hear the angels' song of peace and goodwill. However, the last verse predicts a "golden age" of universal peace and harmony, which Sears believed would follow soon.

Edmund H. Sears

Richard Storrs Willis

It came up-on a mid-night clear, that glo-rious song of old, From

an - gels bend - ing near the earth to touch their harps of gold: "Peace

on the earth, good-will to men, from heav'n's all - gra - cious King!" The

world in sol - emn still - ness lay to hear the an - gels sing.

1. It came upon a midnight clear,
   That glorious song of old,
   From angels bending near the earth
   To touch their harps of gold:
   "Peace on the earth, goodwill to men,
   From heav'n's all gracious King!"
   The world in solemn stillness lay
   To hear the angels sing.

2. Still through the cloven skies they come,
   With peaceful wings unfurled,
   And still their heavenly music floats
   O'er all the weary world;
   Above its sad and lowly plains
   They bend on hovering wing;
   And ever o'er its Babel sounds
   The blessed angels sing.

3. Yet with the woes of sin and strife
   The world has suffered long;
   Beneath the angel-strain have rolled
   Two thousand years of wrong;
   And man, at war with man, hears not
   The love-song which they bring;
   O hush the noise, ye men of strife,
   And hear the angels sing.

4. And ye, beneath life's crushing load,
   Whose forms are bending low,
   Who toil along the climbing way
   With painful steps and slow,
   Take heart, for comfort, love, and hope
   Come swiftly on the wing;
   O rest beside the weary road,
   And hear the angels sing.

5. For lo, the days are hastening on,
   By prophets bards foretold,
   When with the ever-circling years
   Comes round the age of gold;
   When peace shall over all the earth
   Its ancient splendors fling,
   And the whole world send back the song
   Which now the angels sing.

15

O Come, All Ye Faithful

The words to this carol were originally written in Latin as *Adeste Fideles*. They were first published in 1751 by an Englishman named John Wade, who was a music teacher at the Catholic English College in Douay, France. The music for the carol was first published in 1782 by the composer Samuel Webbe. It was not until 1852 that the carol was translated into English by a British minister, Frederick Oakley. The carol is a song of praise that calls upon all believers to celebrate the miraculous birth of the Savior.

John Wade

Samuel Webbe

Majestically

O come, all ye faith - ful, Joy - ful and tri - um - phant, O

come ye, O come ye to Beth - le - hem; Come and be -

hold him, Born the King of an - gels; O come let us a - dore him, O

come let us a - dore him, O come let us a - dore him,___ Christ___ the Lord.

1. O come, all ye faithful,
   Joyful and triumphant,
   O come ye, O come ye to Bethlehem;
   Come and behold him,
   Born the King of angels;
   O come let us adore him,
   O come let us adore him,
   O come let us adore him,
   Christ the Lord.

2. God of God,
   Light of Light,
   Lo, he abhors not the Virgin's womb;
   Very God,
   Begotten not created:
   O come let us adore him,
   O come let us adore him,
   O come let us adore him,
   Christ the Lord.

3. Sing, choirs of angels,
   Sing in exultation,
   Sing, all ye citizens of heaven above;
   Glory to God
   In the highest:
   O come let us adore him,
   O come let us adore him,
   O come let us adore him,
   Christ the Lord.

4. Yea, Lord, we greet thee,
   Born this happy morning,
   Jesu, to thee be glory given;
   Word of the Father,
   Now in flesh appearing:
   O come let us adore him,
   O come let us adore him,
   O come let us adore him,
   Christ the Lord.

17

SILENT NIGHT

On Christmas Eve in 1818, the pastor of a small Austrian village was troubled because the church's organ was broken—some mice had eaten through the bellows. The pastor's name was Joseph Mohr, and without the organ, he would not have any music for the midnight mass that night. While on his parish rounds that day, Mohr visited the cottage of a poor family who had just had a baby. He was reminded of the story of Jesus's humble birth, and on his way home, he wrote a poem about it. When he returned to the church, he asked the church organist Felix Gruber to write music to the words he had written so that they could sing them at the Christmas Eve midnight mass. Gruber wrote the music, and that night he played it on a guitar, and sang it with Mohr and the church choir.

J. Mohr

F. Gruber

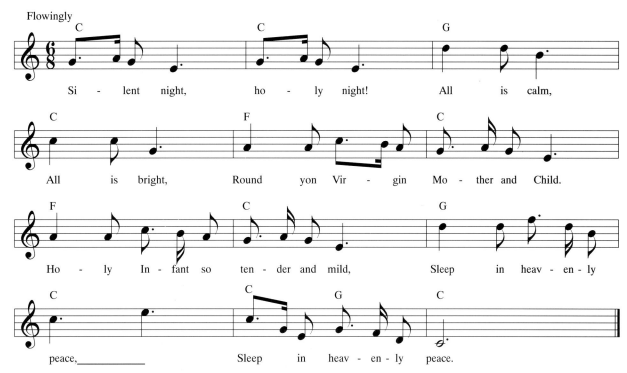

Flowingly

Si - lent night, ho - ly night! All is calm,

All is bright, Round yon Vir - gin Mo - ther and Child.

Ho - ly In - fant so ten - der and mild, Sleep in heav - en - ly

peace,_____ Sleep in heav - en - ly peace.

1. Silent night, holy night!
   All is calm, all is bright,
   Round yon Virgin Mother and Child.
   Holy Infant so tender and mild,
   Sleep in heavenly peace,
   Sleep in heavenly peace.

2. Silent night, holy night!
   Shepherds quake at the sight,
   Glories stream from heaven afar,
   Heavenly hosts sing "Alleluia,
   Christ the Saviour is born,
   Christ the Saviour is born."

3. Silent night, holy night!
   Son of God, love's pure light,
   Radiant beams from thy holy face,
   With the dawn of redeeming grace,
   Jesus, Lord, at thy birth,
   Jesus, Lord, at thy birth.

THE FIRST NOWELL

No one knows who wrote the words and music to this carol, but it is thought to have been written in the 1600s. The origin of the word "nowell" is also uncertain. It may have come from the Latin word "novella," which means "news," and refers to the news of Jesus's birth. "Noël" is the French spelling, but today many people use the Old English spelling, "nowell." This carol tells about the shepherds and the Three Wise Men, who were first to receive the news that Jesus had been born.

The first____ Now - ell the__ an - gels did say, Was to

In fields____ where they lay, keep - ing their sheep, On a

cer - tain poor shep - herds in fields as they lay;

cold win - ter's night____ that was____ so deep:

Now - ell,____ Now - ell, Now - ell, Now - ell,

Born is the King of Is - ra - el!

1. The first Nowell the angel did say,
   Was to certain poor shepherds in fields as they lay;
   In fields where they lay, keeping their sheep,
   On a cold winter's night that was so deep:
      Nowell, Nowell, Nowell, Nowell,
      Born is the King of Israel!

2. They looked up and saw a star,
   Shining in the east, beyond them far;
   And to the earth it gave great light,
   And so it continued both day and night:
      Nowell, Nowell, Nowell, Nowell,
      Born is the King of Israel!

3. And by the light of that same star,
   Three Wise Men came from country far;
   To seek for a king was their intent,
   And to follow the star wheresoever it went:
      Nowell, Nowell, Nowell, Nowell,
      Born is the King of Israel!

4. This star drew nigh to the north-west,
   O'er Bethlehem it took its rest;
   And there it did both stop and stay,
   Right over the place where Jesus lay:
      Nowell, Nowell, Nowell, Nowell,
      Born is the King of Israel!

5. Then did they know assuredly
   Within that house the King did lie,
   One entered in then for to see,
   And found the babe in poverty:
       Nowell, Nowell, Nowell, Nowell,
       Born is the King of Israel!

6. Then entered in those Wise Men three,
   Fell reverently upon their knee,
   And offered there in his presence
   Both gold and myrrh and frankincense:
       Nowell, Nowell, Nowell, Nowell,
       Born is the King of Israel!

7. Between an ox-stall and an ass
   This child truly there born he was:
   For want of clothing they did him lay

All in a manger, among the hay:
    Nowell, Nowell, Nowell, Nowell,
    Born is the King of Israel!

8. Then let us all with one accord
   Sing praises to our heavenly Lord,
   That hath made heaven and earth of nought,
   And with his blood mankind hath bought:
       Nowell, Nowell, Nowell, Nowell,
       Born is the King of Israel!

9. If we in our time shall do well,
   We shall be free from death and hell;
   For God hath prepared for us all
   A resting place in general:
       Nowell, Nowell, Nowell, Nowell,
       Born is the King of Israel!

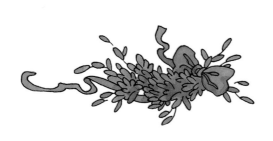

O HOLY NIGHT!

The music for this carol was written in the 1800s by Adolphe-Charles Adam, a Frenchman who was the composer of over fifty operas and ballets, including the famous ballet *Giselle*. The carol celebrates Christ's birth and praises His teachings of love and peace, which brought hope and salvation to the world.

John S. Dwight

Adolphe Adam

O ho - ly night!___ The stars are bright-ly shin - ing, It is the
night of the dear Sav-ior's birth;   Long lay the world___ in sin and er-ror
pin - ing, 'Til he ap - peared and the soul felt its worth.   A
thrill of hope, the wea-ry world re-joic-es, For yon - der breaks a
new and glo-rious morn;___ Fall   on your knees,   O,
hear_____   the an - gel voi - ces! O night_____ di -
vine,_____   O night___ when Christ was born! O night____ di -
vine,_____   O night___ when Christ was born!

24

1. O holy night! The stars are brightly shining,
   It is the night of the dear Savior's birth;
   Long lay the world in sin and error pining,
   'Til he appeared and the soul felt its worth.
   A thrill of hope, the weary world rejoices,
   For yonder breaks a new and glorious morn;
   Fall on your knees, O hear the angel voices!
   O night divine, O night when Christ was born!
   O night divine, O night when Christ was born!

2. Led by the light of faith serenely beaming,
   With glowing hearts by his cradle we stand.
   So, led by light of a star sweetly gleaming,
   Here came the wise men from Orient land.
   The King of Kings lay thus in lowly manger,
   In all our trials born to be our friend;
   He knows our need, our weakness is no stranger;
   Behold your King! Before him lowly bend!
   Behold your King! Before him lowly bend!

3. Truly he taught us to love one another,
   His law is love, and his gospel is peace;
   Chains shall he break, for the slave is our brother,
   And in his name all oppression shall cease.
   Sweet hymns of joy in grateful chorus raise we,
   Let all within us praise his holy name;
   Christ is the Lord, O praise his holy name forever!
   His power and glory evermore proclaim!
   His power and glory evermore proclaim!

O Little Town of Bethlehem

The words to this carol were written in 1868 by Phillips Brooks, a Philadelphia pastor. It was inspired by a trip to Bethlehem that he had taken three years earlier. The day after he wrote the words, he asked his organist, Lewis Redner, to set them to music. Redner couldn't think of a melody, so the music was not ready for the Christmas mass. The next night, he woke up with the music in his head and he quickly wrote it down. The carol was performed for the first time on December 27, 1868.

Phillips Brooks

Lewis H. Redner

Peacefully

O lit-le town of Beth-le-hem, how still we see thee lie! A-

bove thy deep and dream-less sleep the si-lent stars go by. Yet

in thy dark streets shin-eth the ev-er-last-ing light; The

hopes and fears of all the years are met in thee to-night.

1. O little town of Bethlehem,
   How still we see thee lie!
   Above thy deep and dreamless sleep
   The silent stars go by.
   Yet in thy dark streets shineth
   The everlasting light;
   The hopes and fears of all the years
   Are met in thee tonight.

2. For Christ is born of Mary,
   And gathered all above,
   While mortals sleep, the angels keep
   Their watch of wondering love.
   O morning stars, together
   Proclaim the holy birth,
   And praises sing to God the King,
   And peace to men on earth.

3. How silently, how silently,
   The wondrous gift is given!
   So God imparts to human hearts
   The blessings of his heaven.

   No ear may hear his coming,
   But in this world of sin,
   Where meek souls will receive him, still
   The dear Christ enters in.

4. Where children pure and happy
   Pray to the blessed child,
   Where misery cries out to thee,
   Son of the mother mild;
   Where charity stands watching
   And faith holds wide the door,
   The dark night wakes, the glory breaks,
   And Christmas comes once more.

5. O holy Child of Bethlehem,
   Descend to us, we pray;
   Cast out our sin, and enter in,
   Be born in us today.
   We hear the Christmas angels
   The great glad tidings tell:
   O come to us, abide with us,
   Our Lord Emmanuel.

JOY TO THE WORLD

Isaac Watts was one of the greatest hymn writers of all time. He is best known for a collection of poetry called *Psalms of David, Imitated in the Language of the New Testament*, which he published in 1719. The words to this carol are from his version of Psalm 98. It has been said that the music for the carol comes from Handel's *Messiah*, but, there is hardly any similarity between the two pieces, and the identity of the real composer remains a mystery.

Isaac Watts (1674-1748)

Composer unknown

1. Joy to the world! the Lord is come;
   Let earth receive her King;
   Let every heart prepare him room,
   And heaven and nature sing,
   And heaven and nature sing,
   And heaven and heaven and nature sing.

2. Joy to the earth! the Savior reigns;
   Let men their songs employ;
   While field and floods, rocks, hills and plains,
   Repeat the sounding joy,
   Repeat the sounding joy,
   Repeat, repeat the sounding joy.

3. No more let sins and sorrows grow,
   Nor thorns infest the ground;
   He comes to make his blessings flow
   Far as the curse is found,
   Far as the curse is found,
   Far as, far as the curse is found.

4. He rules the world with truth and grace;
   And makes the nations prove
   The glories of his righteousness,
   And wonders of his love,
   And wonders of his love,
   And wonders, and wonders of his love.

WE THREE KINGS OF ORIENT ARE

The words and music to this carol were written by the American John Henry Hopkins, Jr., and were first published in 1862. The song tells of the wise men of the Bible who brought gifts to the infant Jesus. In the Bible, they are not called kings, they are not named, and there are not even three of them. However, it is usually said there were three kings named Melchior, Caspar, and Balthazar. Melchior's gold is a symbol of royalty; Caspar's frankincense is a symbol of divinity; and Balthazar's myrrh represents death, foreshadowing Christ's own death on the cross.

John Henry Hopkins, Jr.   John Henry Hopkins, Jr.

Like a processional

We three kings of O - ri - ent are; Bear - ing gifts we tra - verse a -

far. Field and foun - tain, moor and moun - tain, fol - low - ing yon - der star:

O,___ star of won - der, star of night, star with roy - al beau - ty bright,

West - ward lead - ing, still pro - ceed - ing, Guide us to thy per - fect light.

1. We three kings of Orient are;
   Bearing gifts we traverse afar.
   Field and fountain, moor and mountain,
   Following yonder star:
   > *O star of wonder, star of night,*
   > Star with royal beauty bright,
   > Westward leading, still proceeding,
   > *Guide us to thy perfect light.*

2. Melchior:
   Born a king on Bethlehem plain,
   Gold I bring, to crown him again,
   King forever, ceasing never,
   Over us all to reign:
   > *O star of wonder, star of night,*
   > Star with royal beauty bright,
   > Westward leading, still proceeding,
   > *Guide us to thy perfect light.*

3. Caspar:
   Frankincense to offer have I,
   Incense owns a deity nigh;
   Prayer and praising, all men raising,
   Worship him, God most high:

4. Balthazar:
   Myrrh is mine; its bitter perfume
   Breathes a life of gathering gloom;
   Sorrowing, sighing, bleeding, dying,
   Sealed in the stone-cold tomb:
   > *O star of wonder, star of night,*
   > Star with royal beauty bright,
   > Westward leading, still proceeding,
   > *Guide us to thy perfect light.*

5. All:
   Glorious now behold him arise,
   King and God and sacrifice,
   Heaven sings alleluia,
   Alleluia the earth replies:
   > *O star of wonder, star of night,*
   > Star with royal beauty bright,
   > Westward leading, still proceeding,
   > *Guide us to thy perfect light.*

O star of wonder, star of night,
Star with royal beauty bright,
Westward leading, still proceeding,
Guide us to thy perfect light.

31

DECK THE HALL

This joyful tune is an old Welsh melody. The words are traditional and no one seems to know where they come from. The composer Mozart used the melody in a duet for violin and piano.

Traditional Welsh

Old Welsh Carol

1. Deck the hall with boughs of holly,
   Fa la la la la, la la la la,
   'Tis the season to be jolly,
   Fa la la la la, la la la la.
   Don we now our gay apparel,
   Fa la la, la la la, la la la,
   Troll the ancient Yuletide carol,
   Fa la la la la, la la la la.

2. See the blazing Yule before us,
   Fa la la la la, la la la la,
   Strike the harp and join the chorus,
   Fa la la la la, la la la la.

Follow me in merry measure,
   Fa la la, la la la, la la la,
   While I tell of Yuletide treasure,
   Fa la la la la, la la la la.

3. Fast away the old year passes,
   Fa la la la la, la la la la,
   Hail the new, ye lads and lasses,
   Fa la la la la, la la la la.
   Sing we joyous all together,
   Fa la la, la la la, la la la,
   Heedless of the wind and weather,
   Fa la la la la, la la la la.

O CHRISTMAS TREE
(O TANNENBAUM)

This German carol was brought to England in the nineteenth century by Queen Victoria's husband, Prince Albert, who was German. Having Christmas trees is also said to have been introduced into England by Albert. No one knows who wrote the words or the music for this carol.

Traditional German   Traditional German

Slowly and evenly

O Christ - mas tree, O Christ - mas tree, With faith - ful leaves un -

chang - ing. Not on - ly green in sum - mer's heat, But

al - so win - ter's snow and sleet, O Christ - mas tree, O

Christ - mas tree, With faith - ful leaves un - chang - ing.

1. O Christmas tree, O Christmas tree,
   With faithful leaves unchanging.
   Not only green in summer's heat,
   But also winter's snow and sleet,
   O Christmas tree, O Christmas tree,
   With faithful leaves unchanging.

2. O Christmas tree, O Christmas tree,
   Of all the trees most lovely.
   Each year, you bring to me delight
   Gleaming in the Christmas night.
   O Christmas tree, O Christmas tree,
   Of all the trees most lovely.

3. O Christmas tree, O Christmas tree,
   Your leaves will teach me also,
   That hope and love and faithfulness
   Are precious things I can possess.
   O Christmas tree, O Christmas tree,
   Your leaves will teach me also.

35

I Saw Three Ships

There are many legends about ships arriving with good tidings. In this carol the good tidings are the arrival of Christ and his mother Mary. Both the music and the words are from England and no one knows who wrote them.

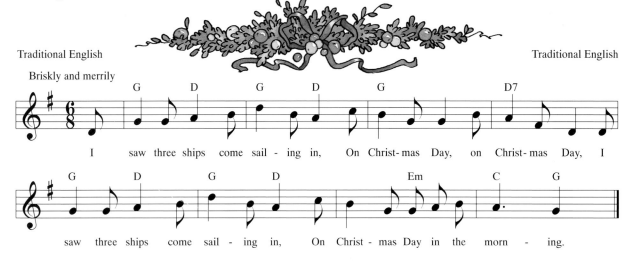

Traditional English

Traditional English

Briskly and merrily

I saw three ships come sail-ing in, On Christ-mas Day, on Christ-mas Day, I

saw three ships come sail - ing in, On Christ - mas Day in the morn - ing.

1. I saw three ships come sailing in,
   On Christmas Day, on Christmas Day,
   I saw three ships come sailing in,
   On Christmas Day in the morning.

2. And what was in those ships all three?
   On Christmas Day, on Christmas Day,
   And what was in those ships all three?
   On Christmas Day in the morning.

3. Our Savior Christ and his lady.
   On Christmas Day, on Christmas Day,
   Our Savior Christ and his lady.
   On Christmas Day in the morning.

4. Pray, whither sailed those ships all three?
   On Christmas Day, on Christmas Day,
   Pray, whither sailed those ships all three?
   On Christmas Day in the morning.

5. O, they sailed into Bethlehem.
   On Christmas Day, on Christmas Day,
   O, they sailed into Bethlehem.
   On Christmas Day in the morning.

6. And all the bells on earth shall ring,
   On Christmas Day, on Christmas Day,
   And all the bells on earth shall ring,
   On Christmas Day in the morning.

7. And all the angels in heaven shall sing,
   On Christmas Day, on Christmas Day,
   And all the angels in heaven shall sing,
   On Christmas Day in the morning.

8. And all the souls on earth shall sing.
   On Christmas Day, on Christmas Day,
   And all the souls on earth shall sing.
   On Christmas Day in the morning.

9. Then let us all rejoice amain!
   On Christmas Day, on Christmas Day,
   Then let us all rejoice amain!
   On Christmas Day in the morning.

Away in a Manger

The music for this carol was probably written by James R. Murray. He first published it in 1887 with a note saying: "composed by Martin Luther for his children, and still sung by German mothers to their little ones." So it became known as "Luther's cradle hymn." We now know that this is false and that the carol is not from Germany. The first two verses come from a poem published in 1885 in a book called *The Little Children's Book*, but no one knows who wrote them. The last verse was added later and its author is also a mystery.

Anonymous

William J. Kirkpatrick

Slowly and evenly

A - way in a man - ger, no crib for a bed, The lit - tle Lord
Je - sus laid down his sweet head. The stars in the sky_____ looked
down where he lay, The lit - tle Lord Je - sus, a - sleep on the hay.

1. Away in a manger, no crib for a bed,
   The little Lord Jesus laid down his sweet head.
   The stars in the sky looked down where he lay,
   The little Lord Jesus, asleep on the hay.

2. The cattle are lowing, the baby awakes,
   But little Lord Jesus, no crying he makes.
   I love thee, Lord Jesus, look down from the sky,
   And stay by my cradle till morning is nigh.

3. Be near me, Lord Jesus; I ask thee to stay
   Close by me forever, and love me, I pray.
   Bless all the dear children in thy tender care,
   And fit us for heaven, to live with thee there.

39

THE TWELVE DAYS OF CHRISTMAS

No one really knows the origin of this song, and there are many different versions. The twelve days of Christmas are the twelve days after Christmas, ending in Epiphany, January 6th, traditionally the day that the wise men arrived in Bethlehem. In many countries that is the day that gifts are exchanged, and in some places gifts are given on each of the twelve days. This is a complicated song to sing, and if you make a mistake when singing it, you are supposed to pay for it.

Traditional English   Traditional English

Gaily

On the first day of Christ-mas, My true love sent to me A par-tridge___ in a pear

tree.   On the se-cond day of Christ - mas, My true love sent to me

Two   tur - tle doves,   and a par - tridge___ in a pear   tree.

1. On the first day of Christmas,
   My true love sent to me
   A partridge in a pear tree.

2. On the second day of Christmas,
   My true love sent to me
   Two turtle doves and a partridge in a pear tree.

3. On the third day of Christmas,
   My true love sent to me
   Three French hens, two turtle doves . . .

4. On the fourth day of Christmas,
   My true love sent to me
   Four calling birds, three French hens . . .

41

On the fifth day of Christ-mas, my true love sent to me   Five   gold_____

rings!   Four___ call - ing birds,   Three   French   hens,

Two___ tur - tle doves,   And   a   par - tridge___ in a pear   tree.

On   the   sixth   day   of Christ - mas, my   true love sent   to   me

Six   geese   a - lay - ing,   Five   gold_____   rings!

5. On the fifth day of Christmas,
   My true love sent to me
   Five gold rings! Four calling birds,
   Three French hens, two turtle doves,
   And a partridge in a pear tree.

6. Six geese a-laying . . .

7. Seven swans a-swimming . . .

8. Eight maids a-milking . . .

9. Nine ladies dancing . . .

10. Ten lords a-leaping . . .

11. Eleven pipers piping . . .

12. Twelve drummers drumming . . .

42

GOD REST YOU MERRY, GENTLEMEN

This is a traditional English tune, probably from London. The tune is thought to be older than the words, which are also traditional. The first line of the carol means "May God keep you in good spirits, Gentlemen."

43

Traditional English   Traditional English

Cheerfully

God rest you mer-ry, gen-tle-men, Let no-thing you dis-

may, Re-mem-ber Christ our Sav-ior, Was born on Christ-mas

Day; To save us all from Sa-tan's pow'r When we were gone a-

stray; O___ tid-ings of com fort and joy, com-fort and

joy, O___ tid-ings of com fort and joy.

44

1. God rest you merry, gentlemen,
   Let nothing you dismay,
   Remember Christ our Savior,
   Was born on Christmas day,
   To save us all from Satan's pow'r,
   When we were gone astray:
   O tidings of comfort and joy,
   comfort and joy;
   O tidings of comfort and joy.

2. In Bethlehem, in Jewry,
   This blessed babe was born,
   And laid within a manger,
   Upon this blessed morn;
   The which his mother Mary,
   Did nothing take in scorn:
   O tidings of comfort and joy,
   comfort and joy;
   O tidings of comfort and joy.

3. From God our heavenly Father
   A blessed angel came,
   And unto certain shepherds
   Brought tidings of the same,
   How that in Bethlehem was born
   The Son of God by name:
   O tidings of comfort and joy,
   comfort and joy;
   O tidings of comfort and joy.

4. "Fear not," then said the angel,
   "Let nothing you affright,
   This day is born a Savior
   Of a pure virgin bright,
   To free all those who trust in him

From Satan's power and might."
   O tidings of comfort and joy,
   comfort and joy;
   O tidings of comfort and joy.

5. The shepherds at those tidings
   Rejoiced much in mind,
   And left their flocks a-feeding
   In tempest, storm, and wind,
   And went to Bethlehem straightway
   The blessed babe to find:
   O tidings of comfort and joy,
   comfort and joy;
   O tidings of comfort and joy.

6. But when to Bethlehem they came,
   Where our sweet Savior lay,
   They found him in a manger,
   Where oxen feed on hay;
   His mother Mary kneeling,
   Unto the Lord did pray:
   O tidings of comfort and joy,
   comfort and joy;
   O tidings of comfort and joy.

7. Now to the Lord sing praises,
   All you within this place,
   And with true love and brotherhood
   Each other now embrace;
   This holy tide of Christmas
   All others doth deface:
   O tidings of comfort and joy,
   comfort and joy;
   O tidings of comfort and joy.

DING! DONG! MERRILY ON HIGH

The melody for this song comes from a famous collection of French dances called *Orchésographie*, published in 1588. The title of the dance is "Branle de l'officiel." A "branle" is a rowdy dance where people jump in the air with their feet together. The word "branle" is probably related to the English word "brawl," which shows how rowdy the dance really was. The words were written by G. R. Woodward in the mid-nineteenth century. The Latin words "Gloria, Hosanna in excelsis" mean "Glory on high."

Bright and Lively

Ding! Dong! Mer - ri - ly on high in
heav'n the bells are ring - ing; Ding! Dong! Ver - i - ly the
sky is riv'n with an - gels sing ing.
Glo ~~~ ~~~ ~~~ ~~~ ~~~ ~~~ ~~~ ~~~ ~~~ ~~~
~~~ ri - a, Ho - san - na in ex - cel - sis!

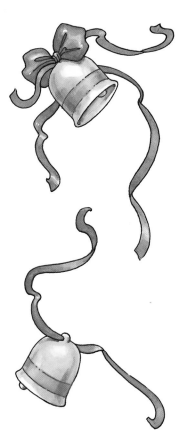

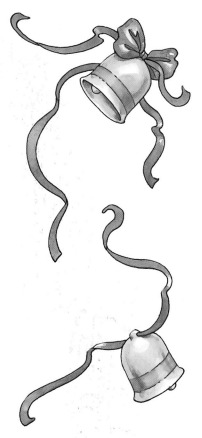

1. Ding! Dong! Merrily on high
   In heav'n the bells are ringing;
   Ding! Dong! Verily the sky
   Is riv'n with angels singing.
       Gloria, Hosanna in excelsis!

2. E'en so here below, below,
   Let steeple bells be swungen,
   And io, io, io,
   By priest and people sungen.
       Gloria, Hosanna in excelsis!

3. Pray you, dutifully prime
   Your matin chime, ye ringers;
   May you beautifully rime
   Your eve-time song, ye singers.
       Gloria, Hosanna in excelsis!

JINGLE BELLS

The words and music to this carol were written by James Pierpont and were first published in 1850. It was originally called "The One Horse Open Sleigh." A lively song about the joys and dangers of sleighing, it doesn't actually mention Christmas, but it is a lot of fun to sing.

Cheerfully

Dash - ing through the snow In a one-horse o - pen sleigh,

O'er the fields we go _____ Laughing all the way; _____ Bells on bob- tail ring, _____

Mak- ing spir - its bright; _____ O what fun it is to sing A sleighing song to- night!

Jin - gle Bells! Jin - gle Bells! Jin - gle all the way! O what fun it is to ride in a

one-horse o - pen sleigh!_____ Jin - gle Bells! Jin - gle Bells! Jin - gle all the way!

O what fun it is to ride in a one - horse o - pen sleigh!

1. Dashing through the snow
   In a one-horse open sleigh,
   O'er the fields we go
   Laughing all the way;
   Bells on bob-tail ring,
   Making spirits bright;
   O what fun it is to sing
   A sleighing song tonight!
      * Jingle Bells! Jingle Bells!
      Jingle all the way!
      O what fun it is to ride
      In a one-horse open sleigh!
      (*repeat)

2. A day or two ago
   I thought I'd take a ride,
   And soon Miss Fanny Bright
   Was seated by my side;
   The horse was lean and lank,
   Misfortune seemed his lot,
   He got into a drifted bank,
   And then we got upsot!
      * Jingle Bells! Jingle Bells!
      Jingle all the way!
      O what fun it is to ride
      In a one-horse open sleigh!
      (*repeat)

WHAT CHILD IS THIS?

The music for this carol is "Greensleeves," a folk melody that has been popular in England for more than four hundred years. Originally the melody was part of a sad love song. The words to the carol were written by William Dix, a businessman and hymn writer who lived in England in the nineteenth century.

William Dix

Old English melody

With slight tension

What child is this,__ who, laid to rest,__ On Mar - y's lap__ is sleep-ing? Whom

an - gels greet with an - thems sweet, while shepherds watch__ are keep - ing?

This, this__ is Christ the King; Whom shep - herds guard and an - gels sing!

Haste, haste to bring him laud, The babe, the son__ of Mar - y!

50

1. What child is this, who, laid to rest,
On Mary's lap is sleeping?
Whom angels greet with anthems sweet,
While shepherds watch are keeping?
This, this is Christ the King,
Whom shepherds guard and angels sing!
Haste, haste, to bring him laud,
The babe, the son of Mary!

2. Why lies he in such mean estate,
Where ox and ass are feeding?
Good Christian, fear, for sinners here
The silent world is pleading.
Nails, spear, shall pierce him through,
The cross be borne for me, for you.
Hail, hail, the Word made flesh,
The babe, the son of Mary!

3. So bring him incense, gold, and myrrh;
Come, peasant, king, to own him.
The King of Kings salvation brings;
Let loving hearts enthrone him.
Raise, raise the song on high,
The Virgin sings her lullaby.
Joy, joy, for Christ is born,
The babe, the son of Mary!

WE WISH YOU A MERRY CHRISTMAS

This humorous English carol is sung by carolers who ask for a reward for their singing, just as carolers do today. Both the words and music are traditional.

Traditional English

Traditional English

1. We wish you a Merry Christmas,
We wish you a Merry Christmas,
We wish you a Merry Christmas,
And a Happy New Year!
Good tidings we bring
To you and your kin;
We wish you a Merry Christmas
And a Happy New Year!

2. Now bring us some figgy pudding,
Now bring us some figgy pudding,
Now bring us some figgy pudding,
And bring some out here!
Good tidings we bring
To you and your kin;
We wish you a Merry Christmas
And a Happy New Year!

3. For we all like figgy pudding,
We all like figgy pudding,
We all like figgy pudding,
So bring some out here!
Good tidings we bring
To you and your kin;
We wish you a Merry Christmas
And a Happy New Year!

4. And we won't go till we've got some,
We won't go till we've got some,
We won't go till we've got some,
So bring some out here!
Good tidings we bring
To you and your kin;
We wish you a Merry Christmas
And a Happy New Year!

53

Angels We Have Heard on High

B oth the words and the melody of this carol are traditional, and were probably written in the eighteenth century. The melody is probably French, though some believe it has its origin in the Canadian province of Quebec. The Latin words "Gloria in excelsis Deo" mean "Glory be to God on high."

Traditional French   Traditional French

Swiftly, joyously

An - gels we have heard on high,_ Sweet - ly sing - ing o'er the plains,

And the moun - tains in re - ply, Ech - o - ing their joy - ous strains.

Glo - ~~~ ~~~ ~~~ ~~~ ~~~ ~~~ ri - a in ex - cel - sis De - o,

Glo - ~~~ ~~~ ~~~ ~~~ ~~~ ~~~ ri - a in ex - cel - sis De - o.

1. Angels we have heard on high,
   Sweetly singing o'er the plains,
   And the mountains in reply,
   Echoing their joyous strains.
   Gloria in excelsis Deo,
   Gloria in excelsis Deo.

2. Shepherds why this jubilee?
   Why your joyous strains prolong?
   What the gladsome tidings be,
   Which inspire your heavenly song?
   Gloria in excelsis Deo,
   Gloria in excelsis Deo.

3. Come to Bethlehem and see
   Him whose birth the angels sing;
   Come, adore on bended knee,
   Christ, the Lord, the newborn King.
   Gloria in excelsis Deo,
   Gloria in excelsis Deo.

4. See him in manger laid,
   Whom the choirs of angels praise;
   Mary, Joseph, lend your aid,
   While our hearts in love we raise.
   Gloria in excelsis Deo,
   Gloria in excelsis Deo.

O Come, O Come, Emmanuel

The words and the music to this medieval carol were discovered in 1856 by Thomas Helmore in a French manuscript in the National Library of Portugal. The first line of each verse calls on Jesus using one of the different titles that He is given in the Bible. This carol, which was written in Latin, was sung in medieval monasteries during the week before Christmas. One verse was sung each night as part of evening prayers.

Slowly, with tension

O come, O come, Em-man - u - el! Red-eem thy cap-tive

Is - ra - el, That in-to ex-ile drear_____ is

gone Far from the face of God's _____ dear son.

REFRAIN

Re - joice! re - joice! Em-man - u -

el Shall come to thee, O Is - ra - el.

1. O come, O come, Emmanuel!
   Redeem thy captive Israel,
   That into exile drear is gone
   Far from the face of God's dear son.
   Rejoice! Rejoice! Emmanuel
   Shall come to thee, O Israel.

2. O come, thou branch of Jesse! Draw
   The quarry from the lion's claw;
   From the dread caverns of the grave,
   From nether hell, thy people save.
   Rejoice! Rejoice! Emmanuel
   Shall come to thee, O Israel.

3. O come, O come, thou dayspring bright!
   Pour on our souls thy healing light;
   Dispel the long night's lingering gloom,
   And pierce the shadows of the tomb.
   Rejoice! Rejoice! Emmanuel
   Shall come to thee, O Israel.

4. O come, thou Lord of David's key!
   The royal door fling wide and free;
   Safeguard for us the heavenward road,
   And bar the way to death's abode.
   Rejoice! Rejoice! Emmanuel
   Shall come to thee, O Israel.

5. O come, O come, Adonai,
   Who in thy glorious majesty;
   From that high mountain clothed with awe,
   Gavest thy folk the elder law.
   Rejoice! Rejoice! Emmanuel
   Shall come to thee, O Israel.

I Heard the Bells on Christmas Day

The words to this carol are from Henry Wadsworth Longfellow's poem "Christmas Bells." Longfellow wrote the poem in 1863 while his son lay wounded, a casualty of the Civil War. The third verse expresses the poet's doubts about the possibility of "peace on earth, good will to men." However, the bells' joyful pealing restores the poet's hopes for peace.

Henry W. Longfellow

Henry Bishop

Sturdily

I heard the bells on Christ - mas Day Their

old fa - mil - iar car - ols play, And wild and sweet the

words re - peat Of peace on earth, good will to men.

1. I heard the bells on Christmas Day
Their old familiar carols play,
And wild and sweet the words repeat
Of peace on earth, good will to men.

2. I thought how as the day had come,
The belfries of all Christendom
Had rolled along th'unbroken song
Of peace on earth, good will to men.

3. And in despair I bowed my head;
"There is no peace on earth," I said,
"For hate is strong and mocks the song
Of peace on earth good will to men."

4. Then pealed the bells more loud and deep:
"God is not dead nor doth He sleep;
The wrong shall fail, the right prevail,
With peace on earth, good will to men."

5. Till ringing, singing on its way,
The world revolv'd from night to day,
A voice, a chime, a chant sublime,
Of peace on earth, good will to men!

INDEX OF FIRST LINES